WATCH YOUR BACK

By

Roberta Barnes

WATCH YOUR BACK

Copyright © 2022 by Roberta Barnes

ISBN: 979-8-9867806-9-6

All rights reserved. No part of this book may be reproduced or transmitted in any form or by any means, electronic or mechanical, including photocopying, recording, or by any information storage and retrieval system, without permission in writing from the copyright owner.

The views expressed in this work are solely those of the author and do not necessarily reflect the views of the publisher, and the publisher disclaims any responsibility for them.

To order additional copies of this book, contact:

Proisle Publishing Services LLC

1177 6th Ave 5th Floor

New York, NY 10036, USA

Phone: (+1 347-922-3779)

info@proislepublishing.com

CONTENTS

Avoiding Violent Crimes	1
Street Sense	4
Jogging and Phone Safety	6
Boat Safety & Security	7
You Are Going on Vacation - Help Burglars Take One Too!	9
Party Safety Tips	11
Commercial (Business) Burglary	13
Protect Yourself From Con-Artists	16
Ten Tips For Safer Emails	18
Holdup Prevention	19
Staying Safe During The Hoilidays	21
Safety While Your Child's Alone	23
Driving Safety	25

Tips For Handling Bogus Phone Calls 26

Tips For Personal Safety 28

What Should You Do To Prevent Sexual Assault 30

Self Defense Tips 32

Tips For Safer Web Browsing 34

Protecting Your Child 36

Property Marking 37

Public Transportation Safety 39

Ensuring a Safe, Clean, and Secure Hotel Room 41

Burglar Prevention 43

Preventing Rape 45

Ten Tips for Avoiding Crime 46

Internet Buying Safety 48
Keeping Your Personal Info Safe 50

Personal Protection Items 52

When You Go un a Vacation 54

Carjacking Tips 56

Atm Security 58

Avoiding Crimes When Parking 61

Charity Fraud 63

The Bank Examiner 64

Tips For Safe Shoping 65

AVOIDING VIOLENT CRIMES

SEXUAL ASSAULT

1. Use initials instead of first names on mail boxes and phone listings.
2. Avoid remaining alone in an apartment laundry room or parking garage.
3. Never admit on the telephone or at the door that you are alone.
4. It is risky to accept a ride home from someone you have just met
5. If you decide to physically resist assault, remember that your goal is to incapacitate the attacker long enough to run to safety and get help
6. If you have been a victim of sexual assault, call police immediately. Do not bathe or change clothes or you may destroy evidence.

ROBBERY

1. When using an automatic bank teller, always be watchful of any suspicious people around you.
2. The chances of being robbed at night are much greater, especially if you are alone.
3. If you find someone waiting and watching outside in the area of an ATM machine, do not use it. Leave the area and report the incident to the police immediately. You could save someone else from being a victim of crime.

STREET SAFETY-USE COMMON SENSE

1. Stay in well lighted, busy areas. Avoid walking alone and avoid known trouble spots.
2. When you carry a purse, hold it close to your body rather than by the handles. Do not wrap purse straps around your wrist, because you can get hurt in a struggle.
3. Carry only what you need in a purse or wallet, not everything you have.
4. Avoid using shortcuts through dark alleys, fields, or vacant lots.
5. If you think you're being followed, cross the street and change directions a few times. Go quickly to a welllighted place with lots of people. Do not go home. You don't want an attacker to know where you live.

- Make sure your home looks like someone is living in it. Don't close your curtains - in daytime this shows the house is empty. Think about getting automatic timeswitches to turn your lights on when it goes dark.
- Fit mortise locks or bolts to all outside doors, and locks to all downstairs or easily accessible windows.
- Cancel any milk or newspaper deliveries.
- Cut the lawn before you go and trim back any plants that burglars could hide behind.
- Get a friend or neighbor to look after your home. They can collect your mail, mow your lawn and so on. This gives the impression that someone is living in your home. If you leave keys with a neighbor, don't label them with your address.

- Don't leave valuables, like your TV, hi-fi or video, where people can see them through windows.

- Mark any valuable items with your postcode and house number using an 'invisible' pen that you can get from DIY shops. If your property is stolen, this will help the police to identify it if it is found, which might not only allow them to return it to you but could also provide them with better evidence to convict the people responsible.

- Do not put your home address on your luggage when you are traveling to your holiday destination.

- Lock the garage and shed with proper security locks, after putting all your tools safely away so they cannot be used to break into your house. If you have to leave a ladder out, put it on its side and lock it to a secure fixture with a 'close shackle' padlock or heavy-duty chain.

- Finally, lock all outside doors and windows. If you have a burglar alarm, make sure it is set and that you have told the police who has the key.

- And just before you set off, it's worth spending a couple of minutes checking that you've done all you had to do and taken everything that you need with you.

HELP FROM YOUR NEIGHBORS

- It's also a good idea to get help from your neighbors. It asks them to keep an eye on your home while you're away.

- You could also ask them to collect post left in the letter box, sweep up leaves, even mow the lawn and generally make the place look lived in.

- You can repay the favor by doing the same for them. Warn the neighbor who has your key not to put your surname, address or even your house number on your keys in case they fall into the wrong hands.

- Is there a Neighborhood Watch scheme where you live? Your local police will tell you if there is a scheme in your area or help you set up one of your own. It could help you keep your home secure while you're away, and has many other crime prevention and community benefits.

STREET SENSE

Wherever you are on the street, in an office building or shopping mall, driving, waiting for a bus or cab, stay alert and tuned in to your surroundings.

Trust your instincts. If something or someone makes you uncomfortable, avoid the person or leave.

Know the neighborhoods where you live and work. Check out the locations of police and fire stations, public telephones, hospitals, and restaurants, or stores that are open late.

- Stick to well-lighted, well-traveled streets. Avoid shortcuts through wooded areas, parking lots, or alleys.
- Don't flash money or other tempting targets like jewelry or clothing.
- Carry a purse close to your body, not dangling by the straps. Put a wallet in an inside coat or front pants pocket, not a back pocket. Carry only what is necessary and try not to keep currency and credit cards all in one place.
- Don't wear shoes or clothing that restrict your movements.

- Have your car or house key in hand before you reach the door.
- Try to use automated teller machines in the daytime. Have your card in hand and don't approach the machine if you're uneasy about people nearby. Better yet, only use the ATM machines inside of grocery store, malls, or gas stations.
- If you think someone is following you, switch direction or cross the street. Walk toward an open store, restaurant, or lighted house. If someone harasses you, don't be embarrassed. Loudly say "Leave me alone! Someone call the police! Get away!"

VEHICLE SAFETY

- Keep your car in good running condition. Make sure there's enough gas to get where you're going and back.
- Always roll up the windows and lock car doors, even if you're coming right back. Check inside and out before getting in.
- Avoid parking in isolated areas. Be especially alert in lots and underground parking garages.
- If you think someone is following you, don't head home. Drive to the nearest police or fire station, gas station, or other open business to get help
- If Someone Tries to Rob You
- Don't resist. Give up your property. Don't risk your life.
- Report the crime to the police. Try to describe the attacker accurately. Your actions can help prevent others from being victims.
- Take a Stand!

- Make your neighborhood and working place safer by reporting broken street lights, cleaning up parks and vacant lots, and lobbying local government for better lighting in public places.
- Initiate a block watch program in your neighborhood by contacting your local crime prevention unit.

JOGGING AND PHONE SAFETY

Jogging Safety:

- Physical Fitness is a major part of military life, but ensure your safety when you exercise alone.
- Jog with a partner.
- Jog in familiar areas, and avoid secluded places.
- Do not jog alone after dark.
- Wear a reflective vest during hours of darkness.
- Carry a whistle when you jog.
- Always lock your door when you leave and carry a key, someone might be waiting for you to leave. Always be aware of your surroundings.

PHONE CALLS:

- Dealing with obscene or annoying phones calls, first thing hang up!
- Do not talk to strangers.
- Do not interview the caller to try to find out who he or she is.
- Do not let your answering machine give you away, that you live alone or are not home.
- Suggested recorded message "Your message is important to me, please leave your name and number". This message does not leave indication that no one is home or that you are alone. Do not use your name on the answering machine.

BOAT SAFETY & SECURITY

Thieves are always on the lookout for easy targets. Don't make yourself an easy target. Always follow these simple steps.

- Never leave anything valuable on display, however small and insignificant it may seem. Thieves steal first and think about value later.
- Don't leave anything loose in the cockpit or on deck.
- Don't leave your engine key in the ignition - always take it with you.
- Keep your boat keys separate from your engine keys.
- Always keep your boat locked when no one is on board, even for a short time.
- Use strong padlocks or rimlocks on all your hatches, entry points and cockpit lockers.

- Constantly check and improve the security on your boat. It's a good idea to fit an alarm and use a visible sticker to say that one is fitted.
- Make sure your cockpit lockers can be properly locked, and check that your main hatch and fore-hatch are strong.
- Also think about having a strongbox down below. If you don't think something is secure, get it fixed.

IMPROVE YOUR SECURITY

Once you've tied up alongside, always do a quick security check before going ashore.

Always:

- Lock anything valuable out of sight in a strong locker secured by a strong padlock;
- Lock up emergency money away from other valuables;
- Keep your curtains closed so that no-one can look in;
- Keep unused ropes, fenders and other items out of sight in your cockpit, lockers and cupboards - and always lock them;
- Make sure that your life raft and outboard motor are secure, as these are valuable and attractive to boat thieves.
- When you go ashore from a dinghy, always remove your oars or paddles, rowlocks or pump, and secure the dinghy with a strong chain and padlock.

- If you are the victim of boat theft, call the police immediately and tell the harbour master or boatyard manager. Check to make sure that your boat is still seaworthy and hasn't been badly damaged.
- And, if you can, check that neighboring boats haven't been broken into as well.
- Get to know other boat owners in your marina and work together to keep the marina secure. You can do the following.
- Keep an eye on other boats, as well as your own.
- Report any strangers at the marina to the harbour master or yard master.
- Don't give your marina access card or key to other people.
- Never tell anyone else the access code to the marina.
- Don't let strangers into the marina, however genuine they may seem.
- Keep the marina gate closed at all times.

YOU ARE GOING ON VACATION - HELP BURGLARS TAKE ONE TOO!

An Empty house is a tempting target for a burglar. Use this checklist of tips to help safeguard your home while you're away.

- Have good locks on all doors and windows and USE THEM!
- Ask a neighbor to watch the house while you're away. It's a good idea to leave your vacation address and telephone number with a neighbor so you can be reached in case of an emergency.

- Never leave your house key hidden outside your home.
- Stop all deliveries, or arrange for a neighbor to pick up your mail, newspapers and packages.
- Arrange for someone to mow your lawn, rake leaves and maintain the yard to give the home a lived-in look.
- Plug in timers to turn lights, a radio or television on and off at appropriate times. This helps to disguise the fact that you are away.
- Don't announce your absence on answering machine messages.
- Leave your blinds, shades and curtains in a normal position. Don't close them unless that is what you do when you are home.
- Close and lock garage doors and windows. Ask a neighbor to occasionally park in your driveway. If you leave your car at home, park it as you normally would. Vehicles parked outside should be moved occasionally to appear that they are being used.
- Tell your local police you plan to be away. Patrol officers may have the opportunity to periodically check your home.
- Engrave your valuables as recommended in Operation I.D. This simple step will allow your stolen property to be identified and returned to you if recovered by the police.

TRAVELING SAFETY

- If you are driving, make sure your vehicle has been properly serviced and is in suitable condition for the journey.

- Try to have specific directions and routes to your destination.
- If you get lost, call the local police for directions or assistance.
- Always keep your vehicle doors and windows locked.
- At stop lights and other traffic delays, leave enough space in front of your vehicle so that you have an escape option in case of an emergency.
- Let someone know the route you intend to travel and your itinerary. This will help authorities in locating you if there is a need to do so.
- Plan your trip carefully and allow for factors such as weather, fatigue, facilities for lodging, food and fuel. Be sure you have sufficient finances, either cash, traveler's checks or credit cards.
- Ask the hotel or motel staff about their security measures so you know what to expect.
- Use the hotel safe to store your valuables during your stay.

PARTY SAFETY TIPS

Whatever your drug of choice, remember: drugs and alcohol can affect your ability to make decisions (such as identifying danger signs and plotting escape routes). Manage how much you consume.

- Always get your own drink. Watch it being poured.
- Don't leave it unattended.
- Don't drink or taste anybody else's drink.

- Don't accept drinks from anyone else
- Dispose of your drink if you think it tastes odd.
- (if you just leave it, someone else may drink it).
- Drugs used to spike drinks can be colorless and tasteless so you might not realize that anything has been added.
- Be aware of the behavior of your friends. Is their behavior out of character? Do they seem too "out of it" for what they've had? See the section on Drink Spiking to find out what to do.
- Watch out for your friends. Are they binge drinking or taking drugs? Are they making safe decisions? Are they OK?
- If your friend needs to sober up or straighten out, check to see that they are OK. Are they alone? Who is with them? Are they safe?
- Encourage people who are drunk to drink water or eat something. Keep an eye on them, if you can.
- Do you really trust whom you are going home with? Are you sure they won't make you do anything you don't want to do? Will they take "NO" for an answer?
- If you are going home with someone different, let someone know. Introduce them to your friends.

IF YOU'RE THROWING THE PARTY

- Know whom you have invited to the party and plan what you will do if there are gatecrashers.
- Provide food and non-alcoholic drink spacers, eg water, soft drinks, juice.
- Keep a look out for your guests. Make sure they're safe and having a good time.

- Offer to organize taxis for your guests. Take a note of the taxi company you have called.
- Create a safe atmosphere. If you know that someone is harassing or intimidating someone else, then do something about it:

1. Let them know you are watching
2. Ask the person to stop;
3. Ask them to leave:
4. Find the victimized person a safe place:
5. Don't be afraid to call the police

State yourself and ask for help if you need it.

COMMERCIAL (BUSINESS) BURGLARY

Ninety percent of burglary prevention is physical security. If your complex is locked up and unauthorized entry is made difficult, time consuming, noisy and visible, chances of a successful burglary are kept to a minimum. The burglar will pass up your business and look for an easier target.

PREVENTION

LOCKS on all outside entrances and inside security doors should be double cylinder deadbolts with moveable collars.

The deadbolt should have at least one inch throw containing a hardened steel insert and protected by a latch guard.

PADLOCKS should be of hardened steel, mounted on bolted hasps and always locked to present exchange. Serial numbers should be filed off to prevent new keys from being made.

DOORS (all outside or security doors) should be of solid construction, metal lined and secured with heavy metal crossbars. Jams around doors must be solid. All exposed hinges should be pinned to prevent removal.

WINDOWS should have secure locks. Burglar-resistant glass treatments are also recommended. An example would be the installation of polyester security film. However, this must be used in conjunction with the alarm's glass break sensor. Heavy metal grates may be used on windows of high vulnerability (such as rear windows). Check with the Fire Marshall for safety requirements.

LIGHTS must provide optimum visibility, both inside and out, with those outside having vandal-proof covers over the lights and power source. Entire perimeter must be well lit, especially the area around doors and other possible entry points.

ALARM SYSTEM should be supplied by a licensed alarm company with a central monitoring station. Check the alarm system on a daily basis, and advertise its presence to deter break-ins.

CASH REGISTER should be kept in plain view from outside the building so it can be easily monitored and should be left open when empty and not in use.

SAFE should be fire proof, burglar resistant, anchored securely and in plain view. Leave it open when it is empty, and use it to lock up valuables when business is closed. Change the combination whenever someone with access to it leaves your employment.

BUILDING EXTERIOR should be checked including the roof, cellar and walls. Secure all openings.

MAINTAIN GOOD VISIBILITY by not allowing landscaping, boxes, trash bins, vehicles or equipment near building where they might provide concealment or access to the roof.

PERIMITER FENCE need to be adequate enough to keep intruders out, and at the same time allow good visibility of your business by neighbors and police (i.e. vertical iron bar fence or 1/8 inch mesh vinyl coated chain link).

KEY CONTROL should be done in a responsible manner. A master key system where one key opens all locks may be convenient, but it may not be the best for security. Code all keys, keep them locked up when not in use, and do not allow employees to leave them lying around or make duplicates. Change locks whenever you suspect key security has been jeopardized.

ID NUMBERS should be marked on all equipment and stickers (such as Operation ID) should be displayed to make this plainly evident to would-be thieves. The best. The best number to use is your personal Florida driver's license number. Also keeping a record of serial number on all equipment may help in recovery.

Protect Yourself from Con-Artists

The con artist's philosophy is "the gullible were put on this earth to be gulled." In the past, con artists were usually referred to as con men. This is no longer the case as more and more women have become involved in con games and numerous variations of con games. Before we proceed with some tips on "how not to get conned" you should always remember that a con artist can be a male or a female. In addition, many times the con artist will work with a child who will assist them in accomplishing their goal. That goal is to GET YOUR MONEY.

Here are some good rules to follow all the time – Whether or not you suspect a fraud:

- Don't believe in something –for nothing offers. You get what you pay for.
- Be suspicious of high pressure sales efforts.
- Take your time; think about it before you part with your money
- Get all agreements in writing. Insist that agreements be in plain English and not legal jargon.
- Read all contracts and agreements before signing. Have a lawyer examine all major contracts.
- Beware of anyone who comes to your door asking for money for charity or for personal reasons.

PREVENTION IMPROVEMENT FRAUD

Home repairs and improvements can be costly. Watch out if

- Somebody offers to do an expensive job for an unusually low price
- If a firm offers to make a "free" inspection or if the person just happened to be in the neighborhood.
- The most popular home improvement frauds are roof repair and painting, driveway sealing, and termite inspection.

To avoid home improvement and repair fraud, try the following:

- Always get several estimates for every repair job, and compare prices and terms. Check to see if there is a charge for estimates.
- Ask your friends for recommendations. Alternatively, ask the firm for references – and CHECK THEM!
- Check the identification of all "inspectors."
- Call the loan consumer Affairs office or the Better Business Bureau to check the company's reputation before you authorize any work.
- Be suspicious of high-pressure sales tactics.

- Pay by check – never with cash. Arrange to make the payments in installments.

TEN TIPS FOR SAFER EMAILS

1. Don't reply to ANY unsolicited emails. Even unsubscribe will alert the senders that your email address is being used.
2. Use your messaging software's filtering tools to reject mail from your frequent spammers' email addresses or with certain words (sex, for example) in the subject line.
3. Find out if your ISP has a spam blocking service. If not, sign up for a third party spam blocking service such as Brightmail (www.brightmail.com).
4. Contact the large directory services such as Bigfoot, Infospace, Switchboard, Yahoo People Search, and whowhere, to tell them you don't want to be listed.
5. Encrypt and digitally sign all your sensitive email messages. If your messaging software doesn't support robust encryption, download PGP Freeware encryption software (http://web.mit.edu/network/pgp.html) and use that.
6. Use WinZip (www.winzip.com) software to compress and password protect your attachments.
7. To avoid cookies sent via email, use email client software, such as Eudora Pro, that lets you shut off its automatic Web Browser rendering engine.
8. Don't read email on a machine that doesn't belong to you or someone you trust. If you use a browser to read email on someone else's machine, use the browser's Clear History tool when you finish to prevent subsequent users from getting into your mailbox.

9. Don't send sensitive personal messages on your work machine.
10. Keep your antivirus software updated at all times.

HOLDUP PREVENTION

- Use the measures outlined in this page.
- Call the police at once if you notice suspicious strangers loitering near or in your place of business.
- Never block the view into your store by crowding display windows. It is important to maintain visibility into your business establishment at all times.
- Secure your teller and cashier operations. Install barriers to keep unauthorized persons out of these areas.
- If practical, mark doorways at varying heights to allow proper identification of robber's height.
- Install a holdup alarm system.
- Install a timed delay switch to turn off exterior lights after your employees have gone for the night.
- Use two people to open and close your business. Establish a system of prearranged signals. One person should stay outside until the other gives the all clear signal.
- Keep cash on the premises to a minimum. Make frequent pickups of money from registers and make regular bank deposits.
- Do not establish a habitual routine when making bank deposits. Robbers will soon learn it.
- Keep the safe in your place of business locked at all times.

- Check the references of job applicants before you hire them.
- In the event you are contacted about an emergency at your business, and the call is of questionable validity, please verify the call with the police dispatcher, before going to your business.

- Have frequent meetings with your employees in order to familiarize them with holdup prevention measures which you have initiated.

IF YOU ARE HELD UP

- Remain calm.
- Do not resist.
- Be identification conscious. Observe the holdup suspect carefully for future identification.
- Report the robbery immediately-dial 911 and don't hang up.
- If possible, protect the crime scene: do not let anyone disturb it. Wait for the police.
- Cooperate with the police. By doing as they request you will help solve the crime.
- Reduce Criminal Opportunity
- and Protect Your Business

STAYING SAFE DURING THE HOLIDAYS

- Even though you are rushing and thinking about a thousand things, stay alert to your surroundings and the people around you. If possible, park your car in an area of high pedestrian activity. Avoid remote areas.
- Lock your car and close the windows, even if you are only gone for a few minutes.

-
- Loose change is a meal for a street person; they will break your window for small change.
- Your cell phone can be sold and reprogrammed and is a sought item of theft.
  A laptop computer will keep a drug user in a high state, at your expense
- Lock your packages out-of-sight in the trunk. Place your valuables in the trunk before you get to your destination, not after, the thief may be watching.
- Be sure and lock your car, many opportunists simply look for unlocked cars.
- If waiting for a ride from a friend or public transportation, do so in busy, well-lit places.
- Consider security film for automobile windows.
- Always report a theft to the police.
- Teach your children to go to the store clerk and ask for help if you become separated while shopping. They should never go to the parking lot or the car alone.
- Avoid carrying large amounts of cash. Pay for purchases with a check or credit card when possible; and if the credit card receipt has carbons, ask for these too. Notify issuers immediately if your credit card is lost, stolen, or misused.
- Be extra careful with purees and wallets. They may become targets for crime in crowded shopping areas, at bus stops, and on public transportation.
- Avoid overloading yourself with packages. It is important to have clear visibility and freedom of motion to avoid mishaps.
- At home, be extra cautious about locking doors and windows when you leave the house, even for a few minutes. Leave lights and a radio or television on so the

- house looks occupied. Do not put large displays of holiday gifts in view of your windows or doors.

- If you go away for the holidays, try to keep your home appearing "lived in": Get an automatic timer for your lights. Have a neighbor watch your home and pick-up your newspapers and mail.
  If you use lights on your tree, make sure that they are in good working order.

- Immediately mark your new gifts with your driver's license number, and note all serial numbers, keeping records in a safe place.

- Remember to be a good friend and neighbor this holiday season: Share these tips with others in your family and neighborhood. Also, why not get your neighborhood together and go caroling. Do not forget the elderly and other people who might be especially lonely during the holidays. Soon, you may wish to form a neighborhood watch group. People helping people, that's what it is all about!

- And lastly, when hosting a party, find alternative transportation for intoxicated guests; and when going out drinking, please remember: Don't Drink and Drive.

SAFETY WHILE YOUR CHILD'S ALONE

Working parents- and that's the majority of American families today- share the anxiety, frustration, and even fear involved in leaving children "on their own" when school lets out, child care arrangements with neighbors and relatives break down, or there simply are not any alternatives.

WHAT CAN YOU DO?

* Make sure your children are ready to care for themselves.
  * Teach them basic safety rules.
* Know where your kids are, what they are doing, and who they are with.

ARE THEY READY? CAN YOUR CHILDREN-

1. Be trusted to go straight home after school?
2. Easily use the telephone, locks, and kitchen appliances?
3. Follow rules and instructions well?
4. Handle unexpected situations without panicking?
5. Stay home alone without being afraid?

Talk it over with them, and listen to their worries and ideas. Work out rules on having friends over household chores, homework, and television. Remember, staying at home alone can build a child's self-esteem, sense of responsibility, and practical skills.

TEACH YOUR "HOME ALONE" CHILDREN

1. How to call 9-1-1 or your area's emergency number, or call the operator?
2. How to give directions to your house in case of an emergency?
3. To check in with you or a neighbor immediately after arriving home.
4. To never accept gifts or rides from people they don't know well. (And you approve of)
5. How to use the door, windows, locks and the alarm system if you have one?
6. To never let anyone into the home without asking your permission.

7. To never let a caller at the door or on the phone know they are alone.
8. To carry a house key with them in a safe place (inside a shirt pocket or sock)-do not leave it under a mat or on a ledge.
9. How to escape in case of fire?
10. To not go into the house apartment if things do not look right- a broken window, ripped screen or opened door.
11. To let you know about anything that frightens them or makes them feel uncomfortable.

DRIVING SAFETY

- Avoid driving alone or at night.
- Keep all car doors locked and windows closed while in or out of your car. Set your alarm or use an anti-theft device.
- If you must shop at night, park in a well-lighted area.
- Avoid parking next to vans, trucks with camper shells, or cars with tinted windows.
- Park as close as you can to your destination and take notice of where you parked.
- Never leave your car unoccupied with the motor running or with children inside.
- Do not leave packages or valuables on the seat of your car. This creates a temptation for thieves. If you must leave something in the car, lock it in the trunk or put it out of sight.

- Be sure to locate your keys prior to going to your car
- Keep a secure hold on your purse, handbag and parcels. Do not put them down or on top of the car in order to open the door.
- When approaching and leaving your vehicle be aware of your surroundings.
- Do not approach your car alone if there are suspicious people in the area.
- Ask mall or store security for an escort before leaving your shopping location

TIPS FOR HANDLING BOGUS PHONE CALLS

They may say that their car has broken down and they need to phone someone for help. They may pretend to be a workman, saying that they need to check your electricity or water. They might even claim to be from the council and that they are carrying out a local survey. Whatever reason a caller gives, you need to be sure that they aren't just trying to get into your home stealing something.

There are around 12,000 incidents of "distraction burglary" each year, where callers get into homes and then steal cash or valuables while the occupier is distracted in some way. Sometimes they work in pairs, with one doing the talking while the other is stealing and they often target the elderly.

Be on you guard every time the doorbell rings, or there's a knock at your door. Look out of your window to see who's there first and if you don't know who the person is. Open the window slightly and talk to them that way, rather than opening your door. Alternatively, have a viewer fitted in your front door so that you can take a good look at who's there first. If your eyesight isn't good, don't worry as you can now get wide-angle viewers to help you see better.

Put the door chain or door bar on before opening the door and talk through the gap. You could even fit a small mirror to the wall next to the door so that you can easily see the person you are talking to. When the caller has left and you've closed the door, don't forget to unhook the chain so that any friend or relative you have given a key to can still get in.

Make sure your back door is locked if someone knocks at your front door. Sometimes thieves work together with one coming in the back way, while the other keeps you talking at the front.

Keeping the chain on the door, ask callers from the council or any other organization to pass through some identification. If you need your glasses to check this don't think it's rude to close the door and go and get them. A genuine caller won't mind. If you're still not sure, ask the caller to leave and tell them to write and make an appointment so that someone else can be with you the next time they call. The basic rule is if you don't know the person at your door don't let them in.

As part of the Government's "Stop, Chain, Check" campaign, local councils, social services and Age Concern centers have further information they can provide to older people. They can also help with door viewers, chains and mirrors, and in certain circumstances, may be able to supply a personal attack alarm that connects through to a control center.

TIPS FOR PERSONAL SAFETY
(Confronting Danger)

- Trust your instincts. If something feels wrong, something is probably wrong.
- Be aware of your surroundings.
- Walk close to the curb, facing oncoming traffic.
- Carry bags close to your body.
- Look confident.
- Tell someone where you are going and when you expect to be back.
- If you are being followed, head for a crowded place.
- If people start milling around you, it could a set-up for a mugging.
- Know yourself, how do you react in a crisis situation? Do you scream, cry, and freeze? How would you defend yourself?
- Remember there is no right or wrong approach to dangerous situations.
- Show your anger, not your fear, a furious reaction often may stop an attack.
- Remember an attacker is looking for an easy victim. Yelling is always a good deterrent (a good choice is to yell FIRE) this will draw attention to those who do not want to get involved but may be concerned for their own safety and may come to help.
- If there are other people around, yell loudly enough to get their attention to what the assailant is doing.
- If you are alone and do not know anyone on the street or nearby, try calling a name out to make the attacker or assailant to believe you may be with someone. This may also help if you are alone at home.
- If someone has a weapon stay calm and wait for an opportunity. Weapons make the situation more

dangerous and difficult, but there still may be something you can do about the situation.

OVERVIEW

Non-resistance to prevent physical violence, Negotiable, Stall for time, Distracting or diverting the assailant, then fleeing, Verbal assertiveness, Screaming, and using a whistle or shriek alarm to attract attention and help.

WHAT SHOULD YOU DO TO PREVENT SEXUAL ASSAULT

- Always be aware of your surroundings
- Stay in well-lit areas as much as possible.
- Walk confidently, directly, at a steady pace. A rapist looks for someone who appears vulnerable.
- Walk on the side of the street facing traffic.
- Walk close to the curb. Avoid doorways, bushes and alleys where rapists can hide.
- If you think you are being followed, walk quickly to areas where there are people and lights. If a car appears to be following you, turn and walk in the opposite direction or walk on the other side of the street.
- Be careful when people stop you for directions or money. Always reply from a distance and never get too close to the car.
- If you are in trouble or feel you are in danger, don't be afraid to attract help any way you can. Scream, yell or run away to safety.
- Always lock your car. Keep your car locked when you are away from it to keep someone from hiding and waiting inside.
- When you are inside the car, lock the doors for safety.
- Look inside and around your car before you get in.
- Be aware of other people in parking areas, especially those close to your vehicle.

- If you think you are being followed, drive to a public place or a police station to get help.
- If your car breaks down, open the hood or attach a white cloth to the antenna. If someone stops to help, stay inside your locked vehicle and ask them to call the police.
- If you choose to carry any type of weapon for self-protection, give careful consideration to your ability and willingness to use it. Remember there is always the chance that it could be taken away and used

Self Defense Tips

Do as much as you can to avoid a confrontation - "anticipation and avoidance" are the key words. If you get caught up in a situation, try to talk to an aggressor without provoking them. Practice relaxation, as appearing fearful or stressed can actually provoke an attack. Remember that body language is important in aggressive situations, so maintain a comfortable distance between you and the aggressor.

Use a gas or electronic attack alarm, as these give out a short piercing sound and will temporarily disorientate an attacker, giving you enough time to escape. Carry it somewhere where you can get to it quickly - - don't leave it buried at the bottom of your bag. If you don't have an alarm, just make a noise yourself by screaming as loud as you can, or shouting "call the police" - if you're loud enough this can be just as effective as a personal alarm. If you have an alarm, use it and shout as well.

Steady yourself if danger threatens. Panic can disable you, so again it's useful to learn how to keep control in a difficult situation. And if you must fight back, adopt what police term the "bash and dash" approach. Primary targets are the eyes, nose, mouth, ears, throat, groin, knees or shins; choose whichever is easiest to get to.

If held from behind don't struggle forward, you'll only exhaust yourself. Instead throw yourself backwards to surprise your attacker or stomp on the lower leg or foot.

You have the right to defend yourself with reasonable force and this includes using items you have with you such as an umbrella, bag, briefcase or keys. However, don't carry or use anything that the law would regard as an offensive weapon. Once you've achieved your primary aim of stunning or surprising your attacker, get away as fast as you can. If you manage to overcome them don't attack again, you could be putting yourself in more danger or you could end up being charged with assault.

These are just very basics of self-defense, but to learn more about it and get some exercise at the same time, find a local self-defense class and encourage your family along to join you. Just remember "anticipation and avoidance" are the best forms of defense.

TIPS FOR SAFER WEB BROWSING

1. Upgrade your Web browser to 128-bit encryption.
2. Read Web site privacy policies carefully and make sure you understand them. Look on your favorite Web sites for privacy seals of approval from BBBOnline, TRUSTe, ePublicEye, or CPA WebTrust.
3. If you're reluctant to provide certain information on an online form, don't.
4. Set up a special free email account with Yahoo, Hotmail, or other free services and supply those addresses when you fill out forms.
5. Before you give your credit card number to any commerce site, make absolutely sure it's secure. Look for a closed padlock icon at the bottom of the screen or https in the URL.
6. Delete all the cookies in your cookie directory (generally c:\windows\cookies) frequently.
7. Disable cookies in your browser (an extreme measure) or set your browser to alert you to cookies, or to accept only cookies that return to their original server or, better yet, install cookie management software (such as Webroot Software's WindowWasher or The Limit Software's CookieCrusher) to control which cookies your PC will accept.
8. Use an anonymous browser such as Anonymizer to hide your identity and filter cookies.
9. If a Web site gives you the option to opt out of tracking, take it.
10. If you have a fast and constant DSL or cable connection, get some personal firewall software, such as Symantec's

Norton Personal FireWall or Network ICE's BlackICE Defender, and install it, FAST!

11. Turn off file and printer sharing in Windows if you're not using it. Intruders will have an easier time accessing your files if this is activated.

12. Elect not to accept news or updates from Web sites you visit.

13. Fake your return address when you use chat or newsgroups.

14. Turn off your Instant Messaging software when you're not using it.

15. Set your Instant Messaging software to allow only people you trust (in your buddy list, for example) to access you.

Protecting Your Child

It has been said that children are our most valuable resources. Therefore, it is absolutely necessary that we take positive measures to insure their safety and prevent them from becoming victims of crime.

Parents...

- Never leave children alone; not at home, in a vehicle, at play, or anywhere.
- Define what a STRANGER is. Let your kids know that just because they see someone everyday (e.g. mailman, paperboy, neighbor, etc.) it does not mean these people are not strangers
- Teach your children the "What if...?" Game, making up different dangerous situations that they might encounter and helping them play out what they would do in that situation.
- Take the time to talk to your children and be alert to any noticeable changes in their behavior or attitude toward an adult or teenager; it may be a sign of sexual abuse.
- Set up procedures with your child's school or day care center as to whom the child will be released to other than yourself, and what notification procedure they are to follow if the child does not show up on time
- Teach your children that thier body is private and no one has the right to touch them in a way that makes them feel uncomfortable. If anyone touches them in a wrong way they should: SAY NO, GET AWAY, and TELL SOMEONE they trust.

Property Marking

Marking your property is one of the most simple and effective ways of protecting your possessions.

- For a start, property marking puts burglars off because it let's others know that the item has been stolen, making it much more difficult to sell. The other big advantage is that it makes tracing and returning your stolen property a lot easier for police.

- For a start, property marking puts burglars off because it let's others know that the item has been stolen, making it much more difficult to sell. The other big advantage is that it makes tracing and returning your stolen property a lot easier for police.

- Make sure you engrave with a fine drill or sharp-pointed tool, and use a template or stencil to keep it neat and tidy. Punching is a form of permanent marking that is done with a hammer and a set of punches bearing numbers and letters. This method is good for bicycles, mowers, engines or other sturdy metal objects, but don't use this on aluminum as it's easily damaged. Of course, you could just improvise and scratch your postcode on it with a sharp object, depending on how happy you expect to be with the final appearance.

INVISIBLE PROTECTION

- Invisible marking is the other method of property marking. This is best for antiques or valuable property that would lose value if spoiled by permanent marking. Police usually check stolen property with a special ultraviolet lamp, so an ultra-violet (UV) marker pen should be used. Just as for permanent marking, use your postcode and mark again if you move. The police also say that it is important to remember that UV marking fades and will need to be renewed every so often.

- Most police forces run schemes that let you borrow an UV or ceramic marker, and you can buy them at most DIY stores. However, in some cases, chemicals can be used to remove invisible marking, and as it fades quickly, you should remember to regularly update your markings.

- Although you can't see it with the naked eye, invisible marking can still be a deterrent to burglars, but you must let them know you've done it by using stickers from the police saying, "property in this home has been marked". Contact your local police for more details about this.

- When it comes to deciding which items to mark, the answer is "up to you". Think about what you value most and what might be attractive to thieves. The truth is almost anything can be a target for theft, so why not mark everything?

- It's worth keeping a property list or inventory of all your household possessions, and be sure to mark the things that you own as you compile your list, including items kept in your shed or garage.

- Finally, where your property is marked is important, especially if engraving or punching. The chances are you'll want to keep the mark out of site, so try marking underneath or around the back of the item. The most important thing to remember is to choose a surface that can't be removed without spoiling the basic appearance or performance of the item. If thieves can't remove your mark without breaking your property, then it's worthless and they probably won't want it.

PUBLIC TRANSPORTATION SAFETY

Public transport is normally very safe and most taxi companies are reputable licensed firms whose drivers have been vetted, so here is some advice that should help you feel more confident when traveling by bus, train, tube or taxi.

ON THE BUS

- Use a bus stop you know is usually busy and is well lit
- Know the departure and arrival times and try and let someone at the other end know which bus you plan to catch. They could always meet you at your stop
- Sit close to the driver. If someone starts up a conversation, be pleasant and confident, but don't give away personal information like where you live or work

BY TRAIN

- Wait on a well-lit section of the platform, close to the exit or where there are other people around. Many stations now have CCTV cameras and staff that are trained to deal with emergencies
- When you get on the train try to sit in a busy compartment and keep any bags and personal possessions you have next to you

- When you get on the train try to sit in a busy compartment and keep any bags and personal possessions you have next to you
- Know where the emergency button or cord is situated or any help points at the station

TAKING A TAXI

- Carry the phone number of a taxi or mini cab firm you know, and whenever you book a taxi ask them for the driver's name and the type of car they will be driving
- Try and book the taxi you need to bring you home before you go out. Give your name and when the driver arrives make sure they know the name it was booked under. If you have to book your taxi in a public place, do it quietly where people are unlikely to overhear your name and address
- If you can, share a taxi with a friend and have your money ready and keys handy at the end of your journey so that you can enter your home quickly
- If ever you feel uneasy in a taxi ask the driver to stop in a busy place that you know well, and get out

Ensuring a Safe, Clean, and Secure Hotel Room

It's a scenario familiar to any business traveller. Your airline flight was delayed, the cab line at the airport was endless and check-in was a mess. Jet lag has struck. It's very late, you're tired and you have a breakfast meeting with a key client at 6:30 AM. You grab your key, avoid the bellman and head to your room to collapse into bed. Stop. Take the next five minutes to perform these safety, security and cleanliness checks and prepare for the next day. These "How to's" will save you time the next morning, they could even save your life someday.

1. When you enter your room prop the door open, turn on the lights, and check the closets, bathroom, under the bed and behind the drapes. Mistakes do happen and sometimes someone else has been assigned to your room. This happens more frequently in suites with adjoining bedrooms that can be sold as separate rooms. Or there could be a thief. In any case, don't close the door until you are sure the room is empty.

2. Check that the connecting doors, windows and sliding doors are locked. In general, avoid first floor rooms with sliding doors.

3. Once you lock the door and attach the safety chain, check the diagram on the back to review the nearest exits and mentally plan your escape route. Look out the door to check that the exit signs are illuminated. If the lights are out, be helpful and contact the front desk to let them know. The few seconds that it takes to review the exit information can save your life in the event of a fire, earthquake or other emergency.
Just do it. FYI, most fire engine ladders can only reach up to the 6th floor.

4. Be sure that the heat or air-conditioner, lights, phone, radio and television are working. Turn on the shower and

sink to check the water pressure and temperature. If they aren't working, switch rooms now. It's not worth waiting for someone to fix the problem, especially late at night.

BURGLAR PREVENTION

What does a BURGLAR like?

Experience has shown us that burglars like many things (mostly other people's things), but two conditions are preferred by most thieves..

- An invitation and
- A fast, easy, undetected entry and exit

Burglary invitations aren't stuffed into envelopes as are birthday party invites; nor do we hang signs in outdoors – "BURGLARS WELCOME" –the way we attach balloons to the mailbox. However, invitations are sent and signs are posted which are equally effective. Have you observed the pile of newspapers or how the mail overflows from your mailbox? Other invites you might recognize include:

- Non-maintained yard.
- Keys left in your vehicle while you run into the store.
- Dark or concealed hiding areas.
- Windows left open when you are away.
- Notes left on exterior doors explaining where you have gone.
- The spare house key on top of the door jam. (Did you think no one knew that key was there?)
- Messages on answering machines stating you are away.

- An open garage door.
- Sliding glass door, without auxiliary locks.
- A house unlit night after night.
- Privacy fence.
- Flimsy door latches and locks.
- Basement windows.

After receiving his invitation the burglar also looks for a quick, undetected entry and exit. He will choose the path of least resistance, which affords him the best chance of getting away without being caught. For this reason, most burglars work the night shift hiding under the cover of darkness. This is an opportunity afforded by nature; other access and escape opportunities, which we provide include:

- A large shrub in front of a window
- A dark alley behind the residence
- A privacy fence around the yard
- An unlocked door or window
- A sliding glass door
- An exterior door without a deadbolt lock

PREVENTING RAPE

If you are in immediate danger of being raped, here are some things that you can do.

Make a loud noise - Carry a whistle or scream "police" to attract attention

Run - Only run if there is somewhere safe to run to. If there is nowhere to go you may aggravate the assailant further by running

Stall – Speak calmly and rationally. Try not to plead, cry or show that you're scared, this may be the reaction that he's going for.

Urinate or vomit – Do anything you can to repulse the assailant. Tell him that you have a STD or AIDS.

Fight - Women who resist attacks and act quickly are less likely to be raped, than those who are passive. The optimum time to react is in the first 20 seconds when the body releases chemicals in the blood that help to put up a fight. Be cautious if he has a weapon.

Keep alert - Even though it will be difficult, try to pay attention to as many details as possible, so that you can identify your assailant.

Get Help – Call 9-1-1 as soon as possible. Police are becoming more willing to help victims of rape. You are not obligated to press charges or go to court.

Collect evidence – Do not Bathe, shower, or douche. If you change clothes put the clothes you were raped in into the bag and seal it.

Tell someone – Call the police, rape crisis counselor, telephone operator, friend. It is very important that someone knows and that it is not kept in secret.

TEN TIPS FOR AVOIDING CRIME

1. Be Alert!
Keep your head up

Be aware of your surroundings.

2. Vary your Routines

Predictability makes you a more likely target

3. Lock it!

Home, car, office – Locks are your first line of defense.

4. Make Your Home a Tough Target

Use floodlights, motion sensors, a security system, deadbolts, etc.

5. Foil Car-Jackers

Keep windows/doors locked, check mirrors and blind spot when stopped. Stay one to one and a half lengths away from the car ahead of you. Sound your horn and flash your lights if you think you're being approached by a car-jacker.

6.   Avoid Car Theft

Lock it!

Use an anti-theft device.

Turn the wheels when you park

Never leave the spare key inside the car.

Park in a well-lighted place, put packages in the trunk

7. Be Creative

Think of unusual ways to protect yourself and your valuables.

8. Be informed

Learn the crime trends in your area and work to protect yourself against them.

9. Get involved

Have you joined or organized a Neighborhood Watch?

10, Don't Give Up!

Crime can be reduced – with action, not apathy

INTERNET BUYING SAFETY

- Despite these many concerns, some now argue that it is actually safer to buy online than buying over the phone or handing your credit card over to someone in a shop. This is because if the online payment is handled properly your banking details will be "encrypted", which means they cannot be viewed by anyone other than those handling the transaction - usually the banks.

- If you're still unsure, Card Watch, the UK banking group that works with the police and retailers to stop credit card fraud, offer the following "top ten tips" when buying online:

- Make sure your web-browser (that's the software that you use to view websites, most commonly Internet

    Explorer or Netscape) is set to the highest level of security notification and monitoring. These options are not always automatically activated when your computer is set-up, so check your manual or the "Help" option.

- Check you are using a recent version of your webbrowser as they often include better security features - up-to-date versions can be downloaded free from the Microsoft or Netscape websites. If you have a different browser or use on-line services such as AOL or CompuServe, contact your ISP (Internet Service Provider) or software supplier to find out how to activate their security features.

- Before purchasing from a website, make a record of the retailer's contact details, including a street address and landline phone number. If these details are not available on the website, consider going elsewhere to buy, do not rely on the e-mail address alone.

- Do not enter personal details unless the security icon is displayed (this is a small padlock that normally appears at the bottom of your browser when you begin your transaction over the Internet). You can click on the padlock to see if the retailer has an encryption certificate. This should explain the type and extent of security and encryption it uses. Only use companies that have an encryption certificate and use secure transaction technology. The address of the page where you enter personal details should also start https://.

- If you have any queries or concerns, telephone the company before giving them your card details to reassure yourself that it is legitimate.

- Print out your order and consider keeping copies of the retailer's terms and conditions and returns policy. Be aware that there may well be additional charges such as postage and VAT. When buying from overseas always err on the side of caution and remember that it may be difficult to seek redress if problems arise.

- Check statements from your bank or card issuer carefully as soon as you receive them. Raise any discrepancies with the retailer concerned in the first instance. If you find any transaction on your statement that you are certain you did not make, contact your card issuer immediately.

- Ensure that you are fully aware of any payment commitments you are entering into, including whether you are instructing a single payment or a series of payments.

- Never disclose your card's PIN number to anyone, including people claiming to be from your bank or the police, and never write it down or send it over the Internet.

- If you have any doubts about using your card, find another method of payment.

Keeping Your Personal Info Safe

- Thieves can use even the most mundane of personal details to help them "verify" that they are someone they aren't, and one of the most common ways of obtaining personal details is "bin-raiding". This is surprisingly common in affluent areas and is spreading out of towns to the countryside; with 75% of local authorities now admitting it happens regularly in their area.

- An exercise carried out with the support of Nottingham City Council and Nottinghamshire Police analyzed the contents of hundreds of household bins to see what people were throwing away. It found that 86% of domestic rubbish contained information helpful to fraudsters.

- Three quarters of the bins that were checked contained the full name and address of at least one person from the household, while 20% of bins contained a bank account number and sort code that could be linked to the name and address of a person from the house.

- So don't keep all of your bills, receipts and other personal documents in an obvious place, if you can lock it away. If you don't have anywhere to lock it, try and keep it somewhere out of the way, or separate it out. Consider investing in a shredder!

- Identity thieves will also try to dupe you into giving personal information either in person, over the phone or by using official sounding e-mails. And of course, personal computers can hold plenty of information useful to fraudsters.

- Be wary. Be suspicious of anyone seeking too much personal information, and don't be afraid to challenge them by asking "why do you need those details?" - A legitimate enquirer won't mind you asking. Make sure you store all important documents and details, such as

your birth certificate, national insurance number, receipts and bank statements, in a safe place.
- Anything containing personal information that you intend to throw out should be destroyed before it is put in the bin. Using a household paper shredder is not taking things too far. If you think you have become the victim of an identity thief, report it to the police, local authority and relevant Government departments or companies immediately.
- Keep personal information in "encrypted" folders on your computer. Encryption scrambles the contents of your chosen folder so it cannot be read by anyone else. You can "unscramble" the contents using a password. Many well-known software companies offer free downloads to help you with encryption, or encryption can be an option under your standard operating system.
- Consider installing "personal firewall" software on your computer to stop online intruders or "hackers" accessing information on your PC.

Personal Protection Items

It seems we all need to carry more of our personal possessions around with us these days.

Cash in your wallet or purse; checkbooks, credit cards, personal organizers and mobile phones are just some of the everyday items that are sorely missed if they are stolen.

All these possessions might seem invaluable, but according to the police the best advice for hanging on to your possessions is "only take what you need with you".

They suggest you to learn minimize the amount of possessions you carry with you. If you don't need a camera with you, don't take it and the same goes for cash and credit cards, only take what cash you need and don't take all your credit cards with you, just the ones you are likely to use.

Keep your purse or wallet somewhere where you can feel it, such as an inside jacket or trouser pocket. Pockets you can zip or button are best. Check every now and then to make sure you still have your wallet or purse on you, but don't make this too obvious as pickpockets can spot you doing this.

Likewise, keep your mobile phone out of sight - in a zipped up pocket is best. If you carry a bag, strap it across your chest and keep hold of it, but at the same time try not to look overly cautious. Keep the zip or opening towards you. Be aware that back-pack style bags are especially vulnerable to thieves.

Do not leave your bag unattended in a public place, such as in a pub, coffee bar or shop. If you're trying on shoes in a shop for example, don't walk even a short distance away from your bag. Keep it with you or ask the shop assistant to hold it for you.

Try to appear relaxed, but at the same time be thoughtful about surroundings, Pick pockets like busy streets and crowded places, and someone bumping into you could well be a pickpocket. If this happens, check you still have your things with you, but again don't make it too obvious that you're doing this.

If something is stolen, go to the nearest police station or call the police. However, don't dial 911 unless you have actually caught someone in the act and have managed to apprehend them. Think carefully before chasing after someone or trying to restrain a thief. The value of what they have stolen may be minor compared to the consequences of being attacked. Always put your own safety first.

WHEN YOU GO ON A VACATION

- One of the times your home is most vulnerable is when it is left empty for an extended period of time. Darkened windows, mail or newspapers collecting and closed windows in hotter weather all advertise your absence to a potential burglar.

- The best protection for your apartment during your absence is to have a house sitter. A friend you trust staying at your house can take care of your pets and/or plants in addition to making sure the house is inhabited.

- Have a neighbor check on your apartment while you're away — turning on lights, radios or TVs and opening and closing curtains will give your apartment the appearance of someone home.

- If you don't have a friend or neighbor to housesit or check your apartment while you're away -- perhaps even if you do — you should keep not only lights but a TV or radio on a timer. If you're like me and have your TV on almost all the time you're home [NOTE: I don't watch it, it's just background noise.], the absence of the sound and that glowing light in the windows announces that you're not there.

- Make sure whoever is checking your apartment while you're away knows how to work your alarm system and who to call in case of a problem.

- Unless you have a house sitter, stop your mail and any newspaper or other delivery. Nothing announces an empty apartment better than a stack of newspapers or an overflowing mailbox. Ask a nearby neighbor to pick up any packages delivered while you're gone.

- If you have a garden or plants on your balcony, make sure someone is watering the plants reguiarly or put the plants where they can't be seen. Plants slowly dying due to lack of water may announce your absence.

- Check your lease. Many landlords require that you notify them if your apartment is going to be left empty for any period of time (this is so they can enter in case of emergency even if they can't reach you). If you've got a house sitter this isn't necessary.

Carjacking Tips

Carjacking of parked vehicles depends on the car owner being inattentive to their surroundings. Carjackers, like street robbers, prefer the element of surprise. Most victims say they never saw the carjacker until they appeared at their car door. To reduce your risk of being carjacked, we have listed some common sense steps below:

- Always park in well-lighted areas, if you plan to arrive/leave after dark.
- Don't park in isolated or visually obstructed areas near walls or heavy foliage.
- Use valet parking or an attended garage, if you're a woman driving alone.
- As you walk to your car be alert to suspicious persons sitting in cars.
- Ask for a security escort if you are alone at a shopping center.
- Watch out for young males loitering in the area (handing out flyers, etc).
- If someone tries to approach, change direction or run to a busy store.
- Follow your instincts if they tell you to walk/run away to a busy place.
- As you approach your vehicle, look under, around, and inside your car.
- If safe, open the door, enter quickly, and lock the doors

- Don't be a target by turning your back while loading packages into the car.
- Make it your habit to always start your car and drive away immediately.
- Teach and practice with your children to enter and exit the car quickly.
- In the city, always drive with your car doors locked and windows rolled up.
- When stopped in traffic, leave room to maneuver and escape, if necessary.
- If you are bumped in traffic, by young males, be suspicious of the accident.
- Wave to follow, and drive to a gas station or busy place before getting out.
- If you are ever confronted by an armed carjacker don't resist.
- Give up your keys or money if demanded without resistance.
- Don't argue, fight or chase the robber. You can be seriously injured.
- Never agree to be kidnapped. Drop the cars keys and run and scream for help.
- If you are forced to drive, consider crashing your car near a busy intersection so bystanders can come to your aid and call the police.
- Call the police immediately to report the crime and provide detailed information.

ATM SECURITY

ATM cash machines have been incorporated in our way of life. They offer a real convenience to those on the run but at the same time offer an element of risk. Using an ATM machine safely requires awareness and a little planning. Just because an ATM machine is open and available 24-hours a day doesn't mean it is safe to use it. Most ATM robberies occur at night between 8:00 PM and midnight. ATM robbers are usually males under 25 years of age and most work alone. ATM robbers usually position themselves nearby waiting for a victim to approach and withdraw cash. Most ATM robbery victims are women and were alone when robbed. Most claim that they never saw the robber coming. Most ATM robbers used a gun or claimed to have a concealed weapon when confronting the victim and demanding their cash.

If your or your family members use ATM cash machines on a regular basis, here are some tips that can make the process a little safer.

- Use only ATM machines in well-lighted, high-traffic areas. Don't use ATM machines that are remote or hidden such as being located behind buildings, behind pillars, walls, or away from public view. Beware of obvious hiding places like shrubbery or overgrown trees. ATM robbers like to have the element of surprise and no witnesses. Robbers like good escape routes like nearby freeway on-ramps or high speed thoroughfares.
- Choose an ATM that looks and 'feels' safer, even if it is a couple of miles out of the way. Try and limit your use to daylight hours. Take someone with you after hours, if you can. When you drive up to an ATM location, scan the area for any suspicious persons. If you see anyone suspicious standing nearby or sitting in a car, drive away. When you approach an ATM on foot be prepared and have your

access card ready. Memorize your personal PIN number to prevent loss and speed the transaction. After inserting your card and your PIN number keep an eye out behind you. Never accept an offer to help or request for help from a suspicious male ahead of you at the machine. If anyone suspicious or seemingly dangerous approaches terminate your transaction and leave immediately, even if it means running away and leaving your ATM card in the machine. First, tell the suspicious male in a loud, firm voice to "back-off" and leave you alone. This is designed to startle the person and give you time to flee, if appropriate. When you receive cash from the machine put it away immediately, extract your card, and walk away.

- If you use your car at a drive-thru ATM machine the same rules apply. Keep the car in gear, with your foot firmly on the brake, while using the ATM machine. Keep a close eye on your rear and side view mirrors during the transaction. Robbers almost always approach from the rear on the drivers side. If you see anyone approaching, drive off even if it means leaving your ATM card behind. If you are confronted by an armed robber, just give up your money without argument. The cash is not worth serious injury or death. Get to a safe place and call the police immediately.
- If lights around the ATM are not working, don't use that machine.
- Avoid ATM machines adjacent to obvious hiding places
- Have your card ready and leave quickly, not counting your cash in public.
- Beware of offers for help from strangers during an ATM transaction.
- Don't fight with or attempt to follow the robber.

- Drive or walk to a safe place and immediately call the police.

Avoiding Crimes When Parking

THEFT AND VANDALISM

- Wherever possible, provide each dwelling with its own locked garage within the property boundaries. Locked garages outside the boundaries or well-lit and visible common car parks are the next best thing.
- Where private garages are not feasible, a car-port or driveway parking is preferable to grouped parking away from dwellings.
- As a general rule, underground or multi-story car parks should be avoided, as they are breeding grounds for vandalism and crime. If they already exist, danger could be minimized by limiting entry points and providing them with sturdy locked gates. Alternatively, each resident could be provided with a lockable garage in their own space, with robust, vandal proof metal doors - garages within garages, so to speak. Or users can be provided with a secure lock or a plastic keycard, which operates electronic doors.
- Grouped car parks should be avoided in high-crime areas. If they cannot be avoided, they should be within view of some dwellings; they should be equipped with sturdy gates or tilt doors, and should never be sited near alleyways.
- Open car parks should be small and within view of dwellings and visitors' car parks should be clearly identifiable, well lit, and visible from dwellings.

RAPE, ASSAULT, ROBBERY

- To make car parks safer, planners should provide direct access from parking areas to the entrance of dwellings.

- Car parks should be no further than 60 meters from dwellings, and the path should be well lit and free from shrubbery.

- Visitors' car parks should be well lit, clearly identifiable, and visible from dwellings.

- Access to enclosed car parks should be limited to residents by some form of electronic entry control device if possible.

- If it is desirable to limit access to dwellings, make sure access via car parks is monitored as well.

- In high-crime areas, advanced technological surveillance methods may be needed in car parks. For example, an infrared unit is available which detects the presence of intruders - but not cats and dogs - by body heat, and automatically switches on all lights in the car park and turns them off after 15 to 20 minutes.

CHARITY FRAUD

Charity fraud does a lot of harm. The con artist takes advantage of people's good will and takes their cash - money that was meant for people in need. You can make sure that any money you give gets into the right hands. Just remember these tips when somebody asks you for a donation.

- Ask for identification - the organization AND the solicitor. Find out what the purpose of the charity is and how funds are used.
- Ask if contributions are tax deductible.
- If you're not satisfied with the answers-don't give.
- Give to charities that you know.
- Check out the ones you've never heard of before, or others whose names are similar to a well-known charity.
- Don't fall for high-pressure tactics. If solicitors won't take no for an answer,- tell them NO anyway - BUT DON'T GIVE THEM YOUR MONEY.
- Be suspicious of charities that only accept cash.
- Always send a check made out to the charity and not the individual requesting the donation.

THE PIGEON DROP

A person approaches you and says that he just found a large amount of money. What should he do with it? Maybe his "boss" can suggest something. He then leaves to check with his "boss" and comes back a few minutes later. His boss said to divide the money, but first, each of you must put up some, "good faith money". Once you hand over your share, you'll never see it or the con artist again.

THE BANK EXAMINER

A con artist will contact you and tell you he is a bank official or police officer and that he needs your help to catch a dishonest bank teller. All you have to do is withdraw your savings and give the money to him so he can check the serial numbers. IF you do, you've been "stung". A real bank official would NEVER ask you to withdraw your money.

Is it hard to believe that people fall for such tricks? Con artists may be the greatest actors you'll ever meet. The pigeon drop and the bank examiner schemes are two of the most successful con games around. Don't be fooled. CALL THEIR BLUFF BEFORE IT"S TOO LATE.

Tips for Safe Shoping

- Shop during daylight hours whenever possible. If you must shop at night, go with a friend or family member.
- Dress casually and comfortably.
- Avoid wearing expensive jewelry.
- Do not carry a purse or wallet, if possible.
- Even though you are rushed and thinking about a thousand things, stay alert to your surroundings.
- Avoid carrying large amounts of cash.
- Pay for purchases with a check or credit card when possible.
- Keep cash in your front pocket.
- Notify the credit card issuer immediately if your credit card is lost, stolen or misused.
- Keep a record of all of your credit card numbers in a safe place at home.
- Be extra careful if you do carry a wallet or purse. They are the prime targets of criminals in crowded shopping areas.
- Avoid overloading yourself with packages. It is important to have clear visibility and freedom of motion to avoid mishaps.
- Beware of strangers approaching you for any reason. At this time of year, "con-artists" may try various methods of distracting you with the intention of taking your money or belongings.

www.ingramcontent.com/pod-product-compliance
Lightning Source LLC
LaVergne TN
LVHW010611070526
838199LV00063BA/5138